MW00412586

THERE IS MORE
You're Not Done Yet

Karen L. Scales

Dee,
Your joy and peace is
is infectuous, Bless you
in your writing.
Karen Scales

Copyright © 2017

By Karen L. Scales

DEDICATION

This book is dedicated to you, Mama.

I also dedicate it to my Father God, Lord and Savior, Jesus Christ who gave me courage and hope. To the Holy Spirit, who nudges my heart to write and who inspired the material in this book.

To my husband Chuck, though a man of few words, his encouragement is loudly heard.

To my sisters and brothers. All five of them!

ACKNOWLEDGEMENTS

To my husband Chuck, thank you for listening to me read my drafts and for your idea to make a book of them.

I also want to give a special thank you to my daughters, Tonya and Andrea, affectionately called my right and left hand, for suggestions, editing and constant support. Thanks to my son Frank for proof reading, also to my son Keith for encouraging me.

My appreciation also goes to my author-friend Sandee L. Hemphill for brainstorming ideas with me. To my sister girlfriends Carolyn, Regelia, and Linda – thanks for your encouragement.

Thanks to Apostle Ron G. Hairston and Pastor Theresa Hairston, for your confidence in me.

Table of Contents

—⟨⟨&⟩⟩—

PREFACE

A late bloomer doesn't have to be a person older in years. A late bloomer is a person who hasn't come into their destiny or bloomed to the fullness of their potential yet – especially when compared to their peer group or to common social expectations.

Many things can delay your progress to your purpose. Putting others before your own pursuits as Ruth did, a failure or bad judgment may have made you detour as it did Moses. It could be a career change that sets you back to the starting line like Amos.

There is so much more to you than anybody knows! There is so much more FOR you that I wrote this book to encourage your faith and help you to go on to the next thing that God has for you.

See yourself in these stories, answer the questions at the end of each chapter to help remove some of the obstacles that have kept you stuck. As you will see in the lives of the late bloomers of this book, time doesn't determine your arrival. With God, you are always on time.

My prayer for you as you journey through these pages is that you realize your wonderful uniqueness. And recognize God's commission to move forward and become who He designed you to be.

> *Now unto Him that is able to do exceeding abundantly above all that we ask or think, according to the power that worketh in us. Ephesians 3:20 (KJV)*

INTRODUCTION

Like many, and perhaps like you, I am a late bloomer. I didn't begin to discover my true self, my potential, talents and capabilities or even my value until later in life.

In the early spring when days are still nippy with a winter chill, daffodils break through the once cold hard ground. Sometimes as early as March before all the snow is completely melted the tulips pop up in a hopeful display. They seem to smile at me shouting a message of cheer "Winter is over! Spring is here!"

Throughout the spring and summer we get to enjoy all types, sizes and colors of blossoms emerging. Before long, fall is announcing its presence: cooler temperatures and trees turning from green to shades red and gold.

It seems like the time for flowers is long past as shades of brown begin to show in the landscape. And here comes the fall blooming Asters, Crocus, Toad Lilly, Chrysanthemum and other late blooming flowers speaking for themselves "There is more. I have beauty to share with you"

In the Midwest of the United States, even in cold, snowy weather, I have seen these late bloomers standing strong and sturdy and bursting with a powerful array of colors: oranges, purples, bronzes, reds, yellows; a variety with a mixture of hues.

I have a heart for Chrysanthemums and all the other late blooming flowers, and for people who, like the flowers, have something to contribute to the world. Because the truth is this: like you and me, the wait through spring and summer isn't a mistake. The Chrysanthemums aren't late at all! It's simply that their season has not come yet.

I want to encourage you to begin to reset and prepare for the coming transformation into a life that is fulfilled and bursting with color. Maybe you're just getting started, or maybe you need the encouragement to carry on. Whatever the case may be, my hope, prayer, and belief is that as we explore the lives of some late bloomers, characters from my favorite book, the Bible, you will grow the confidence to live out your potential.

I believe the stories of these late bloomers will motivate you, as they have motivated me time and time again. May these words bring out the best that is already within you. It's your season!

RUTH
Selfless and Responsible

THE STORY – Life Disrupted

Have you ever been so committed to someone
or something that it caused a delay in pursuing
your own destiny? A tragedy or some event
can happen and because of your commitment,
you deny your plans in order to help another.
If you are a parent, you can probably relate to
this scenario. Your children's needs often come
before yours.

Ruth was that type of person. She married a
man that had come to her town of Moab. I
believe that Mahlon was different from the
other men in Ruth's hometown. He had
traveled to Moab from Bethlehem because of
famine in his country. He was a gentle man of
faith and tender toward his mother. Ruth was

1

attracted to him and his lifestyle. She wanted to spend her life with him.

Mahlon's family, his mother, father and brother, were a close-knit group. They were special in their reverence and love toward a God that Ruth did not know. Ruth became a vital part of this family and she actually loved and respected her mother-in-law, Naomi.

Ruth was a happily married woman for ten years when her husband, Mahlon died before he had lived a long and fruitful life. Ruth's loss left her empty and grieving but Naomi was devastated.

One by one Naomi lost the strength and joy of her life: first her husband, Elimilech, then her son, Chillion, and another son, Mahlon. She didn't even have grandchildren. Naomi wasn't ready for the loud sound of silence in her home. The happy laughter of her man coming in from working all day was gone. No strong men to appreciate the labor of her meals cooked with love. Naomi means pleasant but she said, "don't call me Naomi! Call me Mara." Mara means bitter.

> *But Naomi replied, "Don't call me 'Naomi'! Call me 'Mara'! That's because the Almighty has dealt bitterly with me. Ruth 1:20 (ISV)*

Now, Ruth's husband's death presented good reason and an opportune time for her to leave Naomi and go on with her own life but she was faithful to her mother-in-law.

Naomi urged Ruth and her other daughter-in-law, Orpah, to leave her, get on with their lives, and to marry again. Naomi intended to go back home to her people. They all cried for the loss of their men and the life they all shared together. Orpah followed her advice, kissed her mother-in-law goodbye and went on with her life.

But Ruth was a responsible person and a woman of character. She felt joined to mother-in-law in their grief. She had lost her husband, but Naomi had lost everything. She refused to leave Naomi and allow her to go on that long journey to her homeland alone. She said, "Where you go I will go, and where you stay I will stay. Your people will be my people and your God my God."

PAIN POINT – A Future Sacrificed

Ruth had to sacrifice her life to care for someone else. She was willing – but she had to give up her future, her people and perhaps her dreams, to take care of Naomi. It's a hard choice but people who make such sacrifices, choose what they feel is the "right thing" to do.

She might have felt like "the life that could have been – will never be", because she gave it up for someone else's benefit. Someone she loved.

Through the ages, folks have had to take care of sick family members, younger siblings, older parents or other responsibilities in exchange of their own ambitions. Because of the time it would take away or the money it would cost they couldn't do for themselves and someone else at the same time.

Some feel honored to make the sacrifice. But how many people, over time, feel robbed of their life? Or even embittered feeling "there is not much left for me."

You may have greatly given of yourself but that doesn't mean it's over. You are not empty and sacrifice doesn't mark the end. There is more!

THE TAKE AWAY – Do the Work

Ruth's trip with her mother-in-law back to Bethlehem turned out to be a fresh start for Ruth. Someone noticed her dedication and character as – *she did the work.*

Do you know the story? She went to work in the fields to harvest the grain.

> *And Ruth the Moabitess said to Naomi, "Please let me go to the field and glean among the ears of grain after one in whose sight I may find favor." And she said to her, "Go, my daughter."*
>
> *So she departed and went and gleaned in the field after the reapers; and she happened to come to the portion of the field belonging to Boaz, who was of the family of Elimelech. Ruth 2:2-3 (NIV)*

At first, Naomi and Ruth lived a humble existence. Ruth visited the fields each day to glean food in the fields during the harvest.

Boaz was a wealthy landowner where Ruth went to find grain. He knew her situation and told his workers to leave plenty of grain for her to find. Boaz also encouraged her to work in the safety of his fields only.

Naomi was aware that Boaz was a close relative who, according to Jewish law, had the right to marry the widow Ruth. Naomi encouraged Ruth to go to Boaz

You can read the rest of the love story in the book of Ruth. She married the rich kinsman Boaz and they had a child. Naomi's first grandchild!

Naomi's tragedy was turned to joy and was used in God's greater purpose.

Ruth and Boaz's son whose name was Obed would later become the grandfather of King David, who was also in the lineage of Jesus Christ.

What impresses me about her story is that she did not play the role of a martyr because of her sacrifice. She wasn't a "woe-is-me widow." She didn't believe that it was too late for her.

She continued on to begin again, and she did the work.

I feel a sort of kinship with Ruth in that I was widowed. I spent much time, as a younger mother with four children while my husband was sick. I didn't mind staying with him while he took dialysis treatments for eight years. He was a hero to me.

But life was limited for me. My husband and I tried to make the kids' life as normal as possible, but it was not easy. The day came that he transitioned home to be with the Lord. As a widow, I had to make a decision to do the work to build my destiny without him. I learned many lessons and I found my power, which I want to share with others. I also found my Boaz, or should I say he found me.

What work do you need to do? Do you need to take a course or get a degree? Start sewing again? Get your canvases, paintbrushes and art supplies out of the attic? Get your real estate license? Start that business or ministry? Open that daycare?

It's not too late to take some action, set some goals, make a plan, choose a path, do the work and get out of life – *something for yourself.*

Questions to Answer:

What sacrifices have you had to make for others?

What action have you taken – or do you need to take to begin again for yourself?

What stands out to you about the story of Ruth?

MOSES
Past Mistakes

THE STORY – Rescued for Purpose

You remember the story . . . A Hebrew mother hid her son in a basket that she had made. She laid the basket in the reeds by the river's bank. This courageous woman hid her baby from the danger of a jealous, murderous Pharaoh who was destroying Hebrew male babies.

His maddening fear of the Hebrew people's growth and strength drove the brutal King. He commanded his people to kill the male newborns when they came out of the womb. And he ordered them to heave every one of them into the river. But God had a purpose for this child. His hand of protection thwarted the Pharaoh's demonic edict.

When Pharaoh's sister was bathing in the river she saw the basket hidden near the riverbank. Her maidservant brought the basket to her. She opened it and saw the tender child as he cried out. And her heart was moved with compassion for him.

The baby's sister was standing by, watching, waiting to see what would happen to the child. She quickly volunteered to find someone who could nurse the baby for Pharaoh's sister.

Moses' natural mother became his nanny. The Pharaoh's sister paid her to nurse him and take care of the adopted baby Moses, not knowing that she gave birth to him. His natural mother raised him, and undoubtedly instilled in him the values of his heritage, because although raised in the Egyptian Pharaoh's house, he identified with his people, the Hebrews.

> *And the child grew, and she brought him to Pharaoh's daughter, and he became her son. So she called his name Moses, saying, "Because I drew him out of the water." Exodus 2:10 (NKJV)*

In his early adult years it would seem like Moses had it made and his future was sure. But all that changed when he murdered a man. He saw an Egyptian beating a Hebrew and he killed the Egyptian trying to defend a fellow Hebrew.

> *And he saw an Egyptian beating a Hebrew, one of his brethren. So he looked this way and that way, and when he saw no one, he killed the Egyptian and hid him in the sand. Exodus 2:11-12 (NKJV)*

Because of this grave mistake, his life went in a whole different direction. He was once a man who had favor and privilege; but now Moses had to run for his life. The witness to his crime exposed him as a killer. When Pharaoh discovered what he had done, Moses would ultimately face his wrath and execution as a murderer.

Moses couldn't stay in Egypt. He was a fugitive. So he fled to a foreign country where he ended up getting married and raising his family. For years he worked hard as a shepherd. But a shepherd's life never changed who he was inside, or his passion for his people. Although he may not have realized it, Moses was born to be a leader and a deliverer.

PAIN POINT – I Blew It

What could Moses have been thinking about his destiny at this point?

Questions and fear of uncertainty may have plagued his mind. What future does he have now? His world had been shaken and his future was uncharted.

Hasty jumbled ideas may have been running wildly through his thoughts: where to go and what to do next? How did things go so wrong when his heart only wanted to do right by his brethren? His dream life was turning into a nightmare. If only he had not taken matters into his own hands by striking the Egyptian!

Moses could have felt like a failure. Maybe he grieved over wasting his life because he didn't develop his potential as a leader. God had provided an awesome opportunity! As a baby, his life had been spared! He was being groomed as one of the royal family.

He had education, influence and access to wealth that could get him the finest of everything. He may have even thought being raised as a royal was the specific path through which God would use him to help God's people. And he missed it!

Moses knew he had lost out because of the ignorance and arrogance of his youth. Not knowing the power of a reckless decision and trying to solve a real problem the wrong way: without God.

Moses may have looked back in his mind's eye. He might have even compared the easier life in Pharaoh's palace to the dry, harsh desert and exhausting work of shepherding. Working as a shepherd had its rewards but it was thankless work. Shepherds were disdained but the job provided for his family's needs. It was nothing compared to craving God's greater purpose for his life.

We can imagine Moses saying in his heart of hearts, "I really blew it. I lost my chance to do great things ... I was born to be more than a shepherd! Is this all there is to my life? Is it really too late? There has to be more!"

And many of us are saying the same thing. *I can't be done yet. I know there's more for me.*

Mistakes, blunders, failures, whatever you call them, we all have made them. Some issues have a greater impact on the future than others. But thank God, He gives second, third, fourth and even more chances. He sees us and He welcomes us to get back on course. To walk out the purpose that He designed for our lives.

TAKE AWAY – The Process

Devastating events may happen in your life and force you onto a different path. However, what seems like a detour may actually be a path of preparation, leading toward a greater purpose. Moses thought he was running away to the desert, but he was actually in a process. During the journey, a true transformation took place in Moses. God, through the sands of time, grinded and polished Moses' character until he was ready to do the job God had for him.

As a result of the process, Moses became humble and yielded to God. One scripture in the bible called him humbler than anyone on earth. This was in a situation where the people that Moses was called to serve with, his brother Aaron and sister, Miriam, rebelliously spoke against him. But Moses didn't argue. He let God defend him.

> *Now Moses was a very humble man,*
> *more humble than anyone else on the*

face of the earth. Numbers 12:3 (NIV)

What a far cry from the overconfident young man who took matters into his own hands! Moses met his greatest opportunity not when he was gung-ho, but at a point after he had some difficult experiences of life behind him. It was not in the palace, but in a desert place that God spoke to him.

The glimpse of flames dancing; the crackling sound of fire coming from a bush grabbed his notice from watching his sheep. God captured his attention through a burning bush that would not burn up but continued to blaze. There, He talked with Moses and gave an assignment. He gave him instructions that contained the power to perform it.

As God would have it, the assignment was the very thing that Moses was trying to accomplish when he made his life-changing mistake! Moses didn't want to be a murderer—he just wanted to help his people. Now his mission was to deliver the children of Israel from Egyptian bondage.

Because he trusted God, Moses conquered many self-limiting beliefs, including a problem with stuttering. The help he felt he needed speaking, God provided in his brother Aaron.

And He said, "Isn't Aaron the Levite your brother? I know that he can speak well. And also, he is on his way now to meet you." Exodus 4:14b (KJV)

Moses went on to passionately lead his people – God's people – to another level of existence – from someone's slaves to God's chosen nation, recognized by the entire world.

Everything Moses needed to fulfill his destiny was already in him or given to him. How about you?

Do you realize that no matter what you've been through you still have potential? You have hidden talent and natural abilities waiting to be developed for God's glory and to benefit other people. I believe that, like Moses, you have not missed your opportunity. What is your passion?

Your passion may not look exactly the same as it did twenty years ago, but the essence of it is still in your heart. Real dreams won't go away. I want to challenge you to move forward and do something about it.

Can you recall your desires? Do you remember who you used to be in the privacy of your heart and your thoughts? Can you describe the desire still stirring in your heart? I call this the "luxury of looking in," or introspection. If you are fuzzy about it, journaling may help you get clarity. Remember what you love, list your successes or write down words that describe who you are and what moves you. Ask a friend. Listen to what others say about your talents.

Is this book your burning bush? Are you ready for a reawakening desire for the thing you wanted to do or the person you wanted to become? Maybe you don't realize this but there are people waiting on you in order to find their freedom, to revive their hope.

You can reset your life. Arrive again at the point of your potential and your passion. Then move forward toward making your dream a reality. It starts with a decision.

Questions to Answer:

Describe any desire that may be still stirring within you – the thing you just can't give up on?

What do you think is holding you back from taking action to accomplish your dream?

What stands out to you about the story of Moses? What parts of his journey – purpose, mistake, pain point, process – remind you of your own journey?

DEBORAH
Coach and Mentor

THE STORY – Multi-talented

Do you know anybody that is good at just about everything they do? They just have the Midas touch; whatever they do turns to gold. God has graced them with gifts and abilities and wisdom. They also have experience from various life situations. Others look to them for their insight.

Deborah was like that. She was a political leader and a prophet. Her discernment was undisputed because God anointed her as a Judge to Israel. The people came to her from surrounding areas for wisdom to settle their disputes and complaints.

She was a wife, a warrior, a governmental leader, a prophet and a poetess – she wrote the victory song of Deborah in Judges chapter 5. Her life made a difference. She impacted the lives of her people and brought freedom from the oppression of their enemy.

Deborah was an initiator; she didn't wait for others to tell her what to do. She listened to her heart and to the revelation God spoke to her. She delivered what He said to the people.

Their enemy had greatly oppressed them and when the children of Israel cried out to God, He gave Deborah specific directions for Barak, Israel's military commander. God told Deborah that He would give him victory over Israel's enemy and their army's commander, Sisera.

> *She sent for Barak son of Abinoam from Kedesh in Naphtali and said to him, "The Lord, the God of Israel, commands you: 'Go, take with you ten thousand men of Naphtali and Zebulun and lead them up to Mount Tabor. I will lead Sisera, the commander of Jabin's army, with his chariots and his troops to the Kishon River and give him into your hands.' ". Judges 4:6-7 (KJV)*

Deborah called Barak and told him the specific location God directed them to meet the enemy in battle, but Barak refused to go unless Deborah went to war alongside him. Unafraid, Deborah went into battle alongside Barak and his 10,000 men. But she told him that, because of his timidity, he would not be honored for the win. Another woman would get credit for the victory against Sisera.

> *She said, "I will surely go with you; nevertheless, the honor shall not be yours on the journey that you are about to take, for the LORD will sell Sisera into the hands of a woman." Then Deborah arose and went with Barak to Kedesh. Barak called Zebulun and Naphtali together to Kedesh, and ten thousand men went up with him; Deborah also went up with him. Judges 4:9-10 (NIV)*

While Barak was chasing the fleeing army, the enemy General Sisera escaped on foot and tried to hide in the tent of Jael, the wife of Heber, the Kenite. Because there was a peaceful relationship between General Sisera's boss – King Jabin of Hezor and Jael's husband, Heber the Kenite.

This brave woman tricked the enemy general by offering her home as a place to rest and by giving him milk and a blanket. He hid in her tent until he drifted off to sleep. While he slept Jael crept quietly beside him with a tent peg and hammer in hand. Jael fiercely drove the tent peg through his temple and killed Sisera, the leader of the army. She was not a wimp!

PAIN POINT – Been There, Done That

Deborah was powerful, well known, gifted, multi-talented, and accomplished. She was a seasoned judge, leader and warrior. She might be tempted to think, "what else is there to aspire to? Where do I go from here?" She had been there, done that, and wore the T-shirt as they say. Deborah had conquered nations, overcome barriers and broken the glass ceiling of her day. Are there no more horizons for her?

Is it possible to have accomplished all that you set out to do and wonder how you can top that – fearful that you can't? You might experience boredom from doing the same things over and over again and there's no excitement. It's not challenging anymore. Or maybe experience a let down that causes you to re-live past victories.

There is something sad about living in the past when there is so much life to live in front of you. I've seen men and women who are in a time warp. You look at them and can tell exactly when they were in their hey-day because of the way they dress, the things they talk about, or because they are not open to learning new things. Some movie stars are prime examples. They are unable to go gracefully into the next phase of life because they are trapped in the past.

Why do some folks hesitate to move forward, to investigate a new adventure? ... Is it fear? Afraid that what's next will send them into obscurity or humiliation? Afraid of being invalidated or being put on the sidelines?

Are you stuck in the success of the past? Are you uninterested in what's behind the next door of life? I'm here to tell you that there is so much more to do, so much more to give. People are waiting on what you have to give. They cannot go to the next level without your example and your counsel to lead them through the path.

TAKE AWAY – Pour Into Someone Else

In addition to all of her roles, we see that Deborah was also a coach and a mentor to others. Even with 10,000 men behind him, Barak may was hesitant to lead his army alone, maybe because he didn't believe in himself without Deborah's coaching. No doubt Deborah's mentoring influence helped Barak reach the place to dispense wise counsel and justice for the people of God. He became the next judge of Israel after Deborah.

Deborah did not need to grasp a name for herself because her wisdom, her history with God, and her achievements spoke for her. She was not interested in popularity, but in the strong, godly leadership of her people. She was not interested in staying on top. In fact, she wanted to see others reach their potential. Rather than becoming frustrated with Barak, she offered him the support he needed. She was also honest with him. She did not hide the fact that his hesitation would have consequences.

I'm sure this is a lesson that stayed with him for the rest of his life. If Deborah was interested only in her status, her career, her position, Barak could not have continued to uphold the legacy God intended. Deborah had every right to give her full attention to her work alone, but she understood the greater value of recognizing others' gifts and using her knowledge, skill, and experience to help others succeed.

Recognizing others' gifts and imparting one's own to them makes me think of the jazz musician Quincy Jones whose musical career spanned decades. He began with his Seattle teenage friend Ray Charles, who interested him in arranging music.

Quincy Jones became a bandleader, a solo artist, a songwriter, a producer, an arranger, a film composer, and a record label executive. His success was not only in music, he has also written books, produced major motion pictures, and helped create television series.

Looking over his career, you can see his ascent as he rose to the top and also notice how he influenced, embraced and raised up other artists and younger talent. He mentored many and collaborated with more. His prolific gifts were overflowing his cup into the lives of dozens of other artists.

The late Maya Angelou was a celebrated author, playwright, actress and poet. Dr. Angelou authored twelve best-selling books among many other great accomplishments. She was one mentored Oprah Winfrey. Oprah said, "She was there for me always, guiding me through some of the most important years of my life."

Dr. Angelou also had a twenty plus year mentoring relationship with Melissa Harris-Perry. Melissa is a professor, talk show host, author, intellectual and the Maya Angelou Presidential Chair at Wake Forest University.

When Melissa was an eighteen-year-old student, Dr. Angelou offered her a job instead of signing her drop slip form for Dr. Angelou's course.

Mentors and coaches are needed and can positively influence the minds and lives of both young and older people. Maya's advice is "mentors have to care." The woman who mentored Maya Angelou took her to a very small black library when she was nine years old and introduced her to poetry. Maya said it was her lifeline.

Is now the time for you to pour out into others? There comes a time to evolve into new pursuits by passing the baton to someone else. Don't let past success stunt your growth.

I don't believe in retirement if it means not producing or not creating or no longer influencing. I am suggesting that you experience the joy of creating growth and seeing people and processes go from one stage of development to the next as you breathe the life of your experiences into those who are teachable.

It could be time for you to mentor, coach, and create warriors, cast vision or to be a kingmaker: a person who brings leaders to power whether they become leaders in their own lives, families, or communities.

You can develop and empower other people through the capability and success that you have achieved. How fulfilling that could be!

Questions to Answer:

Have you ever been stuck in a previous success?

Is there a person or a group that will benefit from your experiences and successes?

What stands out to you about the story of Deborah?

ABRAHAM
Delay Is Not Denial

THE STORY – Time Keeps Passing

Have you ever received an inheritance? I have never received a windfall but I did once inherit some inexpensive, but treasured jewelry, a precious memorial of a loved one. Also, on a couple of occasions I was surprised to receive small sums of money.

An inheritance can be something valuable other than money, property or jewelry. Another word for inheritance is "legacy." People can give us a legacy through their life's example. Do you know anyone that influenced you positively because of the life they lived?

I think that observing the lives of others can enrich our lives. For example, a few entrepreneurs I know had the opportunity to observe a family member, a neighbor, or someone they could see up-close who owned a business. Watching an entrepreneur run their business planted the seed in them to build their own business. We inherit gifts from other people's lives. I call this kind of gift a living legacy.

This late bloomer, Abraham, left us a valuable legacy that continues to live – the example of holding on to faith even though a dream is delayed. Abraham is called the father of faith because he believed God and he waited for a dream to be fulfilled.

God promised to do some great things in Abraham's life and give him abundant blessings. He told Abraham that he would become a father of many nations and that God would give him a promised land, wealth and make him a blessing.

Abraham had the potential inside of him to be what God said he could be and have what God said he could have. Yet, Abraham wasn't perfect. He failed many times and became discouraged, but overall he obeyed God's directions and because he believed it, God credited to his account that he was righteous

Even as Abraham believed God and it was accounted to him for righteousness. Galatians 3:6 (KJV)

He expected that he and his wife Sarah would have a son. However, time kept passing … and passing… and passing. What he expected – his destiny – simply did not happen. He was getting older – too old to have a child.

Although He had not given him the promised son, God did bless him financially. So much so that other nations envied his wealth – abundant cattle, gold, silver, good grazing land, productive wells. Jealous men dumped dirt into the wells that Abraham dug in order to try to stop up the flow of blessings, but to no avail. He and all who lived with him continued to flourish. Abraham was wealthy in so many ways and the object of envy, but he still had NO son. Time kept passing. Abraham had become an old man and he still hadn't gotten his big breakthrough, the one desire of his heart, even after so many years of waiting.

PAIN POINT - Disappointment of Delay

Have you ever known of a young athlete who seemed destined to have a future in sports?

Imagine Jimmy. From pee wee leagues all the way to college, Jimmy was an undisputed all-star. Everyone expected him to make big money in the NFL, but Jimmy did not get drafted. Delayed dreams broke his heart and threatened to break motivation. This kind of disappointing delay has happens with many gifted people like singers, musicians and all kinds of artists. Full of hopes and dreams, they look for a big break that never comes. They give all they've got, doing work of developing their gifts but they become so discouraged by the delay that they give up on dreaming at all. Everyone is not meant to be famous but everyone does have purpose and something to contribute to his or her family and community. Jimmy believed his talent in sports would be the key to his future and it was. He could have spiraled into hopelessness. But holding on to his gifts, Jimmy became a beloved teacher, an influential football coach, and a leader in his community.

Abraham's very persistence – his tenacity is an example to me. Despite the disappointment of delay, he did not give up believing God. He did not give up on what was within him. He knew he was a father and a leader as God had promised although it seemed no son would ever come. He could have thrown up his hands saying, "I've followed God in vain." He could have given up in bitterness, but he didn't even stagger. Abraham kept going. I love the way the Scripture sums it up:

> *He staggered not at the promise of God through unbelief; but was strong in faith, giving glory to God; And being fully persuaded that, what he had promised, he was able also to perform. Romans 4:20-21 (KJV)*

TAKE AWAY - Don't Give Up

Delay does not mean the death of a dream. Have you been waiting too? Does it seem that your break will never come? Don't give up. Don't quit. The potential to become "the father of many nations" was still inside of Abraham. And your dream and abilities are still inside of you.

I remember when I decided to go back to school. I feared I was past my prime – I hadn't been to school in decades! And I found that learning was quite a bit harder than it used to be. I felt like giving up. My schedule was brutal. It seemed as if I was always running and everything I wanted to do required that I first do something else! I needed to learn computer skills; I needed to get a tutor because my math skills were not strong. "This is too hard! The house is a mess! I have four kids that need my attention! I'm too old for this!" Waah, waah, waah I cried. I felt pretty defeated.

One day, as I was standing in line at a fast food restaurant, I was going back and forth in my mind about whether or not to quit school. I saw a minister who was pretty well known around town. I didn't think he knew who I was, but then he came up to me, He asked me how I was doing since being widowed. I told him that I finally had to face that I needed to quit school. I'd given it my best, but I had to admit that it was all too much for me. There in McDonald's, this minister reminded me that despite the slow and frustrating progress that I must keep going. Although I was feeling overwhelmed at the moment, he reassured me that the goal was too important.

More than anything, I felt a release from the guilt of letting some other things fall by the wayside. In order to do the work, in order to finish that leg of the race, I must not stagger now! It was important to finish my degree so that I could enter into the next stage that would ultimately take me to the destiny awaiting me. There was more behind the next door.

Abraham finally became a father decades later than any of his peers. Now that's what I call a *real* late bloomer. The key is that he became a father just as God said, and Jesus was the descendant Abraham could have not imagined. God also promised him that through his seed all nations of the earth would be blessed and we know why:

> *"In your seed all the nations of the earth shall be blessed, because you have obeyed My voice." Gen 22:18 (NAS)*

> *The promises were spoken to Abraham and to his seed. Scripture does not say "and to seeds," meaning many people, but "and to your seed," meaning one person, who is Christ. Gal 3:16 (NIV)*

Abraham was waiting on a son. But the outcome looked different from just becoming a dad. Abraham's delayed dream held infinitely more to contribute to the world than that.

Whether you know it or not, there is a greater purpose hidden in the desire of your heart. Give your desires to God and He will give His desires to you. He deposited potential and gifts in you that are meant to bless the world around you.

What is the **core or the essence** of the desire that you have waited for? Do you want to become a best selling author because you want to be **a thought leader and expand the ideas of others**, own a successful business because you want to **have financial clout to make changes and employ people in the process of pursuing your own destiny**, provide a service to develop children because you **sense the call to mold children's lives to reflect the seed God implanted in them**, become a dancer because you are gifted to **communicate to the hearts of others through movement**, create art forms like painting beautiful pictures or photographing **what your heart sees for people's enjoyment and enrichment**, minister to the homeless, prevent human trafficking because **you have a burden for those whose lives have been hijacked** by the difficulties of this life or by unscrupulous greedy people?

Is the essence of your desire to minister the gospel to the world or a small local assembly because **you are compelled to share the power of God's truth through Jesus Christ**, earn your degree because you feel the responsibility **to develop and grow the gifts and talents that you possess**, be involved in the political arena because **you want to represent the people and craft changes that make a difference,** become a wife/husband and mother/father **to raise someone who influences the world.** Is the essence of your desire **to make people connect, make people laugh, make people healed and whole?** Or is it simply the urge to **express what is deep inside of you?**

Don't give up on it. You can still birth it and be a living legacy that will bring satisfaction to you as you impart seed into others.

Questions to Answer:

What is something you have been waiting for?

What caused you to become discouraged?

What stands out to you about the story of Abraham?

ELIZABETH and ZACHARIAS
Speak Life

THE STORY – Listen To What You Are Saying

Have you ever wanted something so desperately but had a hard time believing that it could happen for you? The fear of not getting what you crave can push you into sabotaging yourself. It can make you give a voice to the doubts and the uncertainties that haunt you. You may find yourself explaining why your desire is impossible, instead of speaking life to your dreams.

The couple we are looking at: Elizabeth and her husband Zacharias desired a child. They had hoped and waited for their request but it looked like they had to be satisfied without children. Elisabeth was barren.

They were ordinary people but they had an extraordinary assignment. What was so extraordinary about them was that they birthed a son when were past childbearing age. To have a baby should have been impossible. Some would think it ridiculous to hope for it but God intervened because he had purpose for them.

Zacharias was a priest who was assigned to duties in the temple. While he was doing his temple job of burning the incense an angel visited him. Evidently they had been praying about wanting a son because the angel said, "Your prayers have been heard." He told Zacharias that his wife, Elizabeth, would have a son and told him to name the child John.

The angel told Zacharias their son would be a forerunner of Jesus, turning the hearts of men back to God. This was a message to rejoice about! Elisabeth was extremely happy about it and said that God had taken away her shame of her barrenness.

> *After these days Elizabeth his wife became pregnant, and she kept herself in seclusion for five months, saying, "This is the way the Lord has*

> *dealt with me in the days when He*
> *looked with favor upon me, to take*
> *away my disgrace among men."*
> Luke 1:24, 25 (NAS)

It was a blessing to have descendants. In those days couples wanted to have children because offspring could make a great difference in the family's livelihood. They could work the fields, tend the herds and help with the daily chores in the home. Children were expected to take care of their parents in old age and carry the family name to the next generation.

But unlike his wife, Zacharias's response to the angel reflected how he saw himself. He said, "I'm an old man and my wife is *well stricken in age.*" Now what kind of talk is that? After the angel Gabriel told him what **God** was going to do? Zacharias was looking at his own inabilities.

> *Zacharias said to the angel, "How*
> *will I know this for certain? For I am*
> *an old man and my wife is advanced*
> *in years." Luke 1:18 (NAS)*

Zacharias must have believed it could happen or he wouldn't have been praying about it. Yet and still, in the presence of God's angel, he was speaking doubt to the promise God gave.

"How will I know this for certain?" Really. This was a huge problem.

The negative words he spoke were not in amazement and wonder, but so critical that God had to shut his mouth until the baby was born. I believe this was done to prevent Zacharias from aborting the blessing with his negative doubting words; the angel silenced him.

> *And behold, you shall be silent and unable to speak until the day when these things take place, because you did not believe my words, which will be fulfilled in their proper time. Luke 1:20 (NAS)*

PAIN POINT - Can't Own Your Success

People won't always encourage you when you do something outside of what is expected or seen as the norm. They don't understand what you are doing or why you are doing it.

If you are trying to create something outside of the typical timing or do something out of the box onlookers may say things to discourage or shame you. But what is most important is *what you say* about your dream.

You may be working on a desire. You have researched it and possibly even wrote out your plan to execute it. But you doubt yourself because you don't see it duplicated by others around you. So you tuck it away and keep it a secret.

You can't speak it into existence because you're afraid of what people will say. You can hardly talk about your dream to those who can help midwife it into existence. I must confess that I have been guilty of this one.

I know the self-talk of resistance: "I haven't been trained for this", "those younger than me are far ahead of me", "I don't have as much time left to invest in this." Because of this *stinkin' thinkin,'* I have opened my mouth to tell of my vision and then downgraded it and played small. But I'm learning to speak life to my dreams. Pay attention to what you are saying. Don't be intimidated by the bigness of your dreams.

TAKE AWAY – Celebrate Your Creation

Your dream already exists inside your mind's eye. Others will see it as you speak it. Share your dream only with people who can receive it and celebrate you. Rejoice and speak life to the dreams and the promises that God has given you. Words are powerful. Believe that you are able to do it.

I had a friend who was always talking about building a house. For years he collected building materials on sale. To some people, it seemed to be wishful thinking. But I knew that he believed he was going to build a house because he talked about it all the time and because he showed some corresponding action. Years passed and he continued to act on his belief – an ornate door, beautiful wood kitchen cabinets, marble tiles... The day came that I actually walked into his vision. The bright green grass lined the long driveway as we parked in the front of the house.

From the ceiling in the entry way hung a crystal chandelier – one of his early finds. There was an intercom system throughout the house. Various bedroom doors lined the hallway. I sat on the shaded deck and relaxed with a cold glass of lemonade. Visitors mingled in the back yard where he and his wife hosted the party. My friend showed us around his manifested vision. It was delightful to see something that was once only in his desire.

Elizabeth and Zacharias birthed their desire. That unlikely baby of their prayers became someone who helped changed the world forever. He was John the Baptist, the forerunner of Jesus Christ. Who are you going to affect when you bring your vision into existence?

Questions to Answer:

Are you excited enough to tell someone about your dream? Who would you like to tell? Write an "elevator speech" or a brief description pitching the dream you are building?

Try reading your elevator speech or pitch aloud. Does your speech come out easily? Which parts do you believe most? Which parts are you still feeling unsure about?

Now, consider one corresponding action you can take toward your dream. Take it!

AMOS
Time for a Career Change

THE STORY – Not My Skillset

Following the reign of King Solomon, the
nation of Israel had become two kingdoms:
Israel in the North and Judah in the South.
Although both kingdoms were peaking with
prosperity, the culture was in upheaval. There
was such oppression of the poor, disobedience
to God's laws and religious hypocrisy that God
was at the end of his patience. Here is where
we meet our man. God needed someone to
deliver a message in the midst of the chaos. So,
He called Amos, a simple shepherd and a
farmer, keeper of sycamore-fig trees.
While caretaking of animals, was important
work, God was calling Amos to a new career:
to prophesy to the nations, including Israel.

Amos, the groundskeeper? Amos, the tree guy? He was not a "professional" prophet by any means.

Amos had not been trained in biblical studies. He wasn't known as teacher or scholar. He didn't have any background that lent itself to preaching or prophetic ministry. Yet, with no credentials from man, he went on to do what God had put in his heart. Amos was deeply troubled by the social injustice rampant in society and the complete disregard for the righteousness of God.

God put the burden of Israel's unfaithfulness, falseness on Amos's heart. Can you imagine a father's heartbreak caused by the betrayal the son he loves? Amos also carried the message of correction if they didn't repent – and that message drove him. Everyone did not receive his message because it was harsh. God was going to judge the nations and Israel for their disobedience.

Amos was from Tekoa, a town in Judah south of Jerusalem. He was a country boy, a plain and humble man, but he stood in his truth and delivered his message to the northern kingdom. There were well known prophets already living in the northern area of Israel. Amos's contemporaries were Isaiah and Hosea. These were "professional" prophets.

Even though they were doing their jobs, Amos was executing his assignment. There was room enough for him even if others didn't think so.

PAIN POINT – Ridiculed for Rising to Your Purpose

Amos was not exactly a popular guy. And his was an unpopular message: it announced the judgment of God. Amaziah, a priest from Israel, did not want to hear it. He was so furious with Amos that he may have implied that Amos was running a scam, only there to make money. He told Amos to go back down south and prophesy.

> Then Amaziah said to Amos, "Get out, you seer! Go back to the land of Judah. Earn your bread there and do your prophesying there." Amos 7:12 (NIV)

That disrespect and anger coming from an authority figure could have scared Amos into abandoning his purpose. This contempt was coming from a respected member of the community who Amos would ordinarily submit to.

> *Then Amos replied to Amaziah, "I am not a prophet, nor am I the son of a prophet; for I am a herdsman and a grower of sycamore figs. "But the LORD took me from following the flock and the LORD said to me, 'Go prophesy to My people Israel.' Amos 7:14 - 15 (KJV)*

But Amos was doing what he was driven to do from within. He didn't choose his purpose but it chose him – a shepherd/farmer turned into a prophet to the nations. He was resented because of his promotion. He couldn't let that deter him because his purpose burned within him.

Have you ever had someone disdain your dream, your purpose or the desires of your heart? They may scoff at you and huff and puff because you have the nerve to want to reach for something higher. Sometimes others will not understand you. There may even be times when others will become downright uncomfortable because the very thing that ignites your fire shines an unwanted light on them.

Like Amos's critics they may ask, "Who does she think she is?" Having your work, ideas, or goals criticized and rejected can sometimes be enough to make you draw back from pursuing your dream or the career change you have felt drawn toward. Especially if the criticism is from someone whom you desire approval.

TAKE AWAY – Own Your Destiny

I know what it is like to change direction and to feel out of my depth. After being widowed I wanted to enroll in a Computer Programming curriculum at a local college. Keep in mind that I was already in my 40s, a Mom of four children and a homemaker. Since I knew little about the path to reaching that goal, I sought out the advice of others including a college career counselor that I considered to be an expert.

I told the career counselor about my dream to become a computer programmer. He listened attentively, and then tried to persuade me to enroll in an administrative or executive secretarial program that was offered at the school. Those are fine destinations, but they were not my desire or my destiny.

I don't think the counselor meant any harm; he just wanted me to succeed. And based on my age and experience, secretarial work made sense to him. But he didn't know who I was or my destiny. To tell the truth, I wasn't so sure myself. But inside of me, I had a sense of what direction I wanted to move toward.

I had been a homemaker, but I needed to be a breadwinner. I knew that I wanted a career that offered stability and growth. I've always leaned toward the sciences and had always been a person who enjoyed learning and taught myself. I had researched the profession and interviewed a few computer programmers. All of the information I gathered reassured me that my dream truly could be a reality. I was looking for guidance from the career counselor, but God was already guiding me. It was time for me to own my destiny; and that still holds true for me today. The end of the story? I did indeed become a computer programmer and worked in the IT industry for twenty years.

Be respectful to those who may not support you but – *shine anyway*! You *absolutely must* own your destiny. If it's time to change your career, then do it! Do it even if the new path is radically different from what you have done up to now or from what others think you should do. Whether it's a well-meaning college counselor, your relatives, peers, enemies, or even your own fears 'trying to keep you in your place,' the truth is, nothing can restrict you once you make a decision to do what is in your heart. Step out on faith and own your destiny and you will reap the satisfaction of owning the successful results. Even if the success isn't exactly as you'd imagined, you will have experienced the strength of rising above the opinion of others. That's freedom!

You may have a ministry or community work that you feel propelled to do. You should get wise counsel, of course, a prayer team and eventually a board of directors to support you in your endeavor. But, like Amos, you cannot always look to others to authorize a concern that is the burden of your heart.

We can all benefit from the model Amos shows us. He didn't have the right "skillset," and he certainly did not have the support of others. Nevertheless, he pressed on with the burden of his heart – his desire to follow the new direction God laid out for him. If you, too, want to follow a new direction, you must go to the next level of your desires:

1. *See yourself differently.* Don't limit yourself, to who you are now, focus on who you can become.

2. *Do something different.* It's not how you feel – you may feel scared, uncertain or unworthy but it's what you do that creates the transformation.

3. *Don't be moved by people's opinion.* Have the courage to own your destiny.

Questions to Answer:

What kinds of opposition have you encountered regarding the decision to pursue your destiny?

How do you need to change your current way of life in order to fulfill your purpose?

What stands out to you about the story of Amos?

CALEB
Still Going Strong

THE STORY - There's No Quit In Me

You may remember when we looked at the life
of Moses, that God chose Moses to deliver the
children of Israel from Egyptian bondage and
lead them on a journey. It was a transition
from slavery in Egypt into a land that God
called a land "flowing with milk and honey."
Because of God's judgments on Egypt, Pharaoh
was forced to let their slaves go. Our person of
interest, Caleb, was one of the young men who
witnessed the great judgments and powerful
miracles that took place during that exodus
from Egypt.

> *So I have come down to deliver them*
> *out of the hand of the Egyptians, and*
> *to bring them up from that land to a*

good and large land, to a land
flowing with milk and honey, to the
place of the Canaanites and the
Hittites and the Amorites and the
Perizzites and the Hivites and the
Jebusites. Exodus 3:8 (NKJV)

The children of Israel were ejected from Egypt but as they traveled to their freedom they came to a dead end. The Red Sea blocked the slaves' escape from Egyptian bondage. Their chance for a new life seemed doomed as they looked at the sea in front of them. To make matters worse, Pharaoh changed his mind and decided that he wanted them back. After all, who was going to do the work? So his army pursued them, their horses galloped, thundering behind them. Their formidable chariots carrying the soldiers to capture and return the servants to their misery. But God revealed His protection and showed His mighty power by opening a path for them to cross in the middle of the Red Sea.

God's people walked through the sea on dry ground with a wall of water on each side of the path. When all were safe on the other side, the path closed and the water rushed back into position where Pharaoh's army was covered and drowned as they chased close behind the children of Israel.

After the children of Israel miraculously crossed the Red Sea, they journeyed toward the good land until they camped at Kadesh in the Desert of Paran. The camp was close enough to get a good look at their new destiny. Caleb was one of ten leaders chosen to go secretly in and check out the land. Moses sent these leaders to explore it before they entered into it.

The ten leaders who traveled the land saw that it was indeed fertile and produced healthy livestock and succulent food. They brought back bunches of luscious fruit as proof of it. Although they had the proof that it was a land flowing with milk and honey, Caleb and Joshua were the only two spies who brought back raving reviews of the richness of the land they saw.

The other eight spies saw not only the good land, but they saw the people that occupied the land. The ten doubting leaders caused the children of Israel to be afraid and killed the people's faith with their report. They talked more about the obstacles (gigantic people in the land) than reporting about the rich land. Their words kept God's people from believing His promise to them.

Unlike Caleb, they saw themselves as grasshoppers in comparison to the people that lived there. They must have held themselves in low esteem as well as God's ability to keep His promise to them. But not Caleb! He wholeheartedly believed God. He encouraged the people to go for it! He assured them that they could take the Promised Land.

> *Then Caleb silenced the people before Moses and said, "We should go up and take possession of the land, for we can certainly do it." Numbers 13:30 (NIV)*

But Caleb's encouragement was not enough to make them take the initiative and move during that window of opportunity. As a result of their unbelief, the children of Israel wandered in the wilderness for more than forty years. And they faced many obstacles in their wanderings. It amazes me that they missed their chance to enter the good land because of unbelief yet they still had to trust God during the forty plus years of wandering in the wilderness.

Caleb was ready to seize the blessing as a young man but because of the people's unbelief that window closed. He had to journey with them in the wilderness until the older unbelieving generation died off.

> *Not one of you will enter the land I swore with uplifted hand to make*

your home, except Caleb son of
Jephunneh and Joshua son of Nun.
Numbers 14:30 (NIV)

Caleb had many experiences from the time they left Egypt to the time they entered the Promised Land. When the land was finally being divided among the tribes, Caleb was right there. Still strong and still no quit in him! Caleb was just as strong in faith, strong in body and strong in spirit as he was forty plus years earlier when he spied out the land.

PAIN POINT – Fewer Opportunities

So, you have great experience and you still have a lot of drive, passion and ideas but opportunities are no longer as open to you as they once were. That can be painful. You want to create and initiate but others don't recognize your value.

Despite the fact that Caleb believed they could take the Promised Land, Caleb's word was disregarded. And he had to suffer along with the rest. Regardless of the truth he brought to the table, no one listened. His word, his experience, his confidence, his expertise all seemed to mean nothing. "Nobody gets it!" His view was not considered.

I must say I can relate to that. When I started working as a computer programmer I was a mature woman and I worked with a lot of young guys. I sometimes felt like an alien from out of space. One guy told me that I was "just different." I later realized that he could not see the "real" me. What he saw was his perception of me.

They just didn't get me! They were looking at the package, my outer appearance. I was not a kid like many of them were. They couldn't see the drive, passion and ideas inside of me that I brought to the table. Although, I knew that I was fresh and I brought a diverse point of view and problem solving approach to the table. In my journey as a late bloomer I have often thought, "I can see you, why can't you see me?"

TAKE AWAY – Create Your Own Space

Now that they have arrived, Caleb wants his slice. In his passion and drive he wholeheartedly expects what God has promised. It is time to claim his space! And he is tough enough to drive out the people in it. The surge of energy he feels stakes his claim, "Give me this mountain!"

> I am still as strong today as the day Moses sent me out; I'm just as vigorous to go out to battle now as I was then. 12"Now then, give me this (mountain) hill country about which the LORD spoke on that day. Joshua 14:11-12b (NIV)

Caleb inherited Hebron, which was a city of a famous giant named Kiriath Arba. Caleb conquered and made Hebron a land free from war by getting rid of the giants. Though it took time, Caleb finally acquired what he proclaimed to the children of Israel when he spied out the land.

Despite the fact that my view and voice was marginalized in the beginning of my career, opportunities to prove myself professionally as a computer programmer and business analyst emerged in time. But sometimes I had to create my own opportunities. Before starting my programming degree, I participated in a program for women in transition. As a graduate of that program, I realized the opportunity to return and encourage other women facing life transitions, including widowhood, divorce and downsizing. Even though my place at work seemed marginal, during my lunch hour I decided to reach out. For years I spoke to different groups of women. Amazingly this volunteer work opened an opportunity to be a guest on the *Oprah Winfrey Show*.

Oprah interviewed women whose lives were changed when they were left to establish themselves without the support of a husband. The show focused on the reality that even though we get married and plan to live happily ever after, there is no guarantee that a husband will be there to provide. The guests were examples of women who pursued employment or business ownership without a spouse. Two of the guests had been deserted by their husbands and left to fend for themselves. There were others that started their own businesses. As a mother of four, widowed at 40, my story was about needing to return to school and become the family breadwinner.

Looking back, I can see that my story has evolved from the "frightened young widow" or "suddenly single mom" to a woman who has tapped into that power within us all – the power that produces your life's vision. The road not been easy, but I am currently an author, speaker and coach with my own business helping women and late bloomers resurrect and reignite their dreams.

What opportunity can you create for yourself? Do you need to launch that business, start that ministry, write that book or get your art supplies or sewing machine out of the basement and refresh your talents? What skills do you have that are lying dormant, that you can use to create revenue or change lives or both?

No one can dictate your destiny. If there is no room made for you, create your own space. You already have the gifts and talents inside of you. Let God guide you through your prayers and your passion.

Questions to Answer:

Has a door to an opportunity closed for you?

How can you use your gifts and talents to create an opportunity for yourself?

What stands out to you about the story of Caleb?

HANNAH
All In!

THE STORY – Strong Desire

Have you ever had a sense of inadequacy when you compared your life's accomplishments to someone else's? Not quite making the grade is a feeling that some late bloomers are familiar with. But it could be just a matter of timing. The characteristic of being a late bloomer is that they manifest their potential later than their peers. Hannah was a late bloomer and one of her peers, Peninnah, harassed her because Hannah seemed to be unproductive. She had not manifested the desire of her heart yet. She desired a child with all her heart.

Hannah was married to Elkanah, who loved her deeply but he acquired another wife,

Peninnah. They lived during Old Testament times when having more than one wife was accepted as the norm. Some commentators think that Elkanah married Peninnah in order to have his children and perpetuate his lineage. Peninnah was like was a fruitful vine. She had ten children by Elkanah.

Elkanah loved Hannah best. He was sensitive to her concerns about being barren and he treated her with exceptional kindness and generosity. Peninnah was Hannah's rival for Elkanah's love and attention. She constantly provoked Hannah in order to make her feel inadequate. She taunted her because Hannah's womb was closed. Peninnah made comparisons between them especially when they were all together as a family.

> But unto Hannah he (Elkanah) gave a worthy portion; for he loved Hannah: but the Lord had shut up her womb. And her adversary also provoked her sore, for to make her fret, because the Lord had shut up her womb. 1 Samuel 1:5-6 (KJV)

Elkanah made a trip every year and took his wives and family to a celebration. The children of Israel were required by God to attend an annual holy event where the people would meet with God in the Tabernacle of congregation at Shiloh. There, they offered peace offerings as a sacrifice of thanksgiving and praise to God.

Year after year Peninnah would give Hannah the blues. Hannah wanted a child so badly that when Peninnah would gloat and twist the knife of accusation in her back, Hannah was so grieved that she couldn't enjoy the feasting of the occasion. It was like a holiday but she was depressed. Hannah was eating the tears of anguish and had no appetite for food. Her husband tried to console her but her desire was too deep and her disappointment too great.

> *This went on year after year. Whenever Hannah went up to the house of the Lord, her rival provoked her till she wept and would not eat.*

> *Her husband Elkanah would say to her, "Hannah, why are you weeping? Why don't you eat? Why are you downhearted? Don't I mean more to you than ten sons?" 1 Sam 1: 7-8 (NIV)*

Hannah had a good life. She was loved and she did not lack for the good things in life. But she had a desire that would not leave her. She desired to give birth. If a dream is in your heart that you have not given birth to, it can nag you and pull at your satisfaction with life. Your craving may not be understood by others or may even be mocked by someone you are in relationship with.

PAIN POINT – Chided and Childless

Hannah had two major problems:

1. She couldn't conceive a child, which was the greatest desire of her heart.

2. She was rejected and taunted by her husband's other wife, Peninnah.

What is so difficult about having an unfulfilled dream is that it is visible to you and others may not see it – or they may notice that you haven't given birth to anything yet. You could feel disrespected and like Hannah even scorned by those who have already birthed their potential. This lagging behind can take the fight right out of you. But when you know deep down inside what you're capable of producing, you cannot let it go.

Hannah would not let it go! Her womb was closed and only God could open it. She became more persistent than ever and gave her request for a child all the focus and fervency that she had. In Shiloh at the temple she prayed so intensely that the priest, Eli, who observed her thought she was drunk.

As she continued praying before the Lord, Eli observed her mouth.

> *Hannah was speaking in her heart;*
> *only her lips moved, and her voice*
> *was not heard. Therefore Eli took her*
> *to be a drunken woman.*
>
> *And Eli said to her, "How long will*
> *you go on being drunk? Put your*
> *wine away from you." But Hannah*
> *answered, "No, my lord, I am a*
> *woman troubled in spirit. I have*
> *drunk neither wine nor strong drink,*
> *but I have been pouring out my soul*
> *before the Lord. 1 Sam 1:12-15*
> *(ESV)*

Her longing was so strong that it became her priority. What other people thought of her did not stop her pursuit. People's lack of confidence in your dream can be used to propel you to produce it!

TAKE AWAY – Take It By Force

Hannah sacrificed to get her desire fulfilled. She was "all in"! What I mean by being "all in" is to be totally commitment, sold out, no holds barred, and one hundred percent focused. While everyone else was feasting, Hannah was fasting and praying like a drunken woman.

She did her part and then let God do what only He could do. Hannah believed God and He rewarded her faith. The son of Hannah's prayer, Samuel, became a great priest, judge and prophet, loved and respected by everyone. He anointed two Kings, Solomon and David, who looked to him for counsel.

I used the subtitle "Take It By Force" because it reminds me of when Jesus said the disciples *"The kingdom of heaven suffereth violence and the violent take it by force" Mathew 11:12b* (KJV). It gives me the sense of warring over what God has provided, what He has placed inside of me. This is what you need to have, the heart of a warrior to war over your dream and TAKE IT!

When we fiercely go against the odds we can do the unexpected!

I recently read about a woman who came from drug addiction and homelessness to graduate from Harvard University with a bachelors' degree in Psychology. Norma Heath is a late bloomer who, because she was "all in", took her dream from a written goal to reality. She had a desire, set goals and fiercely pursued it to the end.

After losing her job, Norma became depressed and entered a downward spiral that left with no stability to live a normal life. At the point of her greatest brokenness, Norma found a woman's shelter called Rosie's Place in Boston, Massachusetts.

Volunteers asked Norma to write down some goals for her life. At first her list consisted of a handful of small things like going to the doctor and staying away from the type of people and lifestyle that brought her down. But she also had the audacity to write as the number one goal on her list, her ultimate dream: to graduate from Harvard University.

Norma was always a strong student but did not have the stability to fulfill her God given potential. The volunteers encouraged her to follow her dream and she did just that! Now that she has completed that goal, she wants to continue to the next level for her Master's Degree. She wants to help others on their journey. She wants to multiply her dream: "I'm thinking about how many lives I'm gonna to touch."

It takes total commitment to have a tenacious grip, holding onto your dream. There will be times the sacrifices seem in vain but it pays off if your all is in the process. Hannah won the ultimate benefit of her persistence. She had two more sons and three daughters.

Indeed the LORD visited Hannah, and she conceived and bore three sons and two daughters. And the young man Samuel grew in the presence of the LORD. 1 Samuel 2:21 (ESV)

Have you ever half-heartedly chased a dream and stopped pushing toward the goal? Like Hannah, you must be "all in!" Whatever it takes; no matter what anybody thinks about you pursuing your desire. Let your second wind carry you; get your last kick in to thrust through the ribbon. There is a reward for persistence and fulfillment at the finish line. When you win, those you are assigned to receive your contribution also win. Even as Hannah's son Samuel was not just her selfish ambition to have children, remember, your gift, talent, dream is not just for you.

Questions to Answer:

How have you experienced pressure from peers?

What prevented you from going "all in" for your dream?

What stands out to you about the story of Hannah?

ABOUT the AUTHOR

Karen L. Scales is an inspirational, motivational speaker, author and coach. She is an ordained minister and regularly speaks at her local assembly, Kingdom Faith International Christian Center (www.kficc.com) in Columbus, Ohio. She is happily married to Chuck and is a proud mother and grandmother.

She believes you should live life to the fullest and leave this life emptied of all God has deposited within you. Karen's desire is to bring out the best that is already in you.

You are invited to join a great Facebook group to join with those who want to live their legacy today.

http://bit.ly/liveyourlegacytoday

To learn more about Karen or how to work with her, visit her website at:

http://karenscales.com

23756165R00052

Made in the USA
Columbia, SC
13 August 2018